A CONVERSATION
WITH JESUS

ON

RELATIONSHIPS

A CONVERSATION
WITH JESUS

ON

RELATIONSHIPS

DAVID HELM

CHRISTIAN
FOCUS

Scripture quotations are from *The Holy Bible, English Standard Version*, copyright © 2001 by Crossway Bibles, a publishing ministry of Good News Publishers. Used by permission. All rights reserved. ESV Text Edition: 2011.

ISBN 978-1-5271-0325-2

Published in 2019

by

Christian Focus Publications Ltd.,
Geanies House, Fearn, Ross-shire,
IV20 1TW, Great Britain

www.christianfocus.com

Cover design and typeset by: Pete Barnsley (CreativeHoot.com)

Printed in China

CONTENTS

TWO WORDS
BEFORE
BEGINNING

ONE

The book in your hands is one of six. Short volumes all. Think of them as people to meet, not pages to be read. In each, a charcoal sketch is drawn of a person who first appeared on the pages of John's Gospel. Both women and men. Real flesh and blood. All worthy of attention. And each one fully capable of standing on their own two feet.

Beyond this, they all have someone in common. Jesus. The Nazarene. The Christ— he who forever changed the world we live in. Anyway, they all met him. In person. And they talked with him. More than that. Each one had a *conversation with Jesus* about something important to them.

TWO

I suppose something should be said about why 'these six'? Let's just say the selection is subjective. Author's prerogative. I liked them. I wanted to know them. And I learned significant things from each one of them. There are good reasons to think that you will connect with them too. Their struggles are our struggles. Their questions too. In fact, some people are saying there has never been another century to resemble the one these six lived in, until ours came along. And if that is the case, you may just run into yourself by running into them.

At any rate, there came a day when they all ran into Jesus. Of course, he is the only character to emerge in every encounter. I am confident that you will enjoy getting to know him.

DIRECTOR'S
NOTES

CAST:

 WOMAN: indeterminate age, modest, energetic but worn

 JESUS: an itinerant teacher, commonly-attired, spirited but fatigued

SETTING:

A well for drawing water. The surrounding terrain is rugged—mountains are far off—but the well is in a deserted spot outside of town. The sun is directly overhead, beating down.

A man, obviously fatigued, is seated beside the well. Sweat is running down his face as heat can be seen rising from the hardened surface of the ground. From the direction of the town, the figure of a woman can be seen. She is alone, but with a water jar upon her head. Upon coming into view, the lines on her face reveal weariness.

treasures. And with his *Century Cycle*, ten plays covering each successive decade of the 20th century, Wilson explores the African American experience like no other. The literary dance penned between characters Jeremy and Mattie is just one instance of his power in revealing the human longing for a relationship of significance. A relationship that promises 'to stay with me'—one that remains.

IN SEARCH OF RELATIONSHIP

In the fourth chapter of the Gospel of John, we meet a woman who shares this same desire for relational intimacy.[2] We are not told her name, but two significant details about her are given. First, the writer tells us that she came from a small town in the region of *Samaria*. Now, admittedly this detail isn't particularly striking, and how it identifies her with us isn't immediately clear.

However, we are helped by what we know of first-century Palestine. At that time, and in that particular part of the world, people fell into one of two groups. From a Jewish perspective, the first was comprised of spiritual insiders: men and women who lived in the south, practiced their religion in Jerusalem, and traced their historical legacy to King David. The other group were outsiders: *Samaritans* who lived in the north, worshiped on Mount Gerizim, and emphasized their connections to Joshua and Jacob. These outsiders thought little of intermarrying with foreigners, believing in many gods, and more generally, trying to make their way in a world that seemed stacked against them in every conceivable way.

That the woman is identified as a Samaritan is an important signal. Like many today, she considers herself a spiritual outsider. Through no fault of her own, she didn't run with the pious crowd and never attended the proper institutions of worship on the 'right side of the tracks.' And we can be sure that others didn't let her forget it.

Having been spiritually marginalized, her prospects for a relationship with God were slim. The best she could hope for in this world was a relationship with a person, someone here, one who understood her and wanted to be with her. This *horizontal plane* would become the realm in which she sought out relational intimacy, support, purpose, and meaning. The woman at the well pursued relationships in the here and now, rather than one with God above.

OUR OWN SEARCH

A second clue connecting her to many of us is how she went about navigating life when God was out of reach. In the story, we learn that she is living with a man. But as the conversation with Jesus unfolds, we will learn that she has been in a relationship with five other men. Five. No big deal. After all, the sexual ethics of the religiously pious are not her concern. She is free to realize herself and create her own happiness in whatever bed she chooses. But, that kind of freedom comes with a cost.

Can we relate to her yet? Absolutely. And we can point to a number of contributing factors. From the times in which we live, to our family history (or lack of it), to our own life choices, there are many things that get in the way of a real connection with God. We don't feel whole. We feel like something is missing. And so we draw our faith from the well of human relationships. We press on regardless of past failures. We keep looking for real connections.

THE SETTING FOR A CONVERSATION ON RELATIONSHIPS

We can imagine the scene. A small, dusty town. Jesus is sitting there, looking tired, exhausted even, and is sprawled out beside a well for drawing water.

> *And he had to pass through Samaria.*
> *So he came to a town of Samaria called*

Sychar, near the field that Jacob had given to his son Joseph. Jacob's well was there; so Jesus, wearied as he was from his journey, was sitting beside the well. It was about the sixth hour.

Even before speaking with the woman at the well, John shows us Jesus. He has arrived ahead of her, and by the looks of it, in need of a rest. It's the sixth hour—or noon—which is the hottest hour of the day. He's perspiring while the ground around him is hard as stone.

Shortly, the woman will approach. And we already know more about Jesus than she does. John has told us that he has come into the world like a sun, like a blinding light ready to bring us back into a relationship with God. But for her, and this fact is important, Jesus is nothing more than a dog-tired traveler trying to make his way home.

We can imagine her entering his space the way we do when coming upon others at a bus stop. They arrived first. Not us. No eye contact is made (at least that is obvious). No words are spoken. And yet, already, we have surmised the sex and race of the one sitting there.

RELATIONSHIP BREAKS THE SILENCE

Jesus is the first one to speak.

> *There came a woman of Samaria to draw water. Jesus said to her, 'Give me a drink.'*

To us, Jesus' first words—'Give me a drink.'—sound offensive. They come off badly. Some might go so far as to call them patriarchal or chauvinistic, the kind of things a man says when trying to assert a measure of power over a woman. Contextually, however, they are not.

> *The Samaritan woman said to him, 'How is it that you, a Jew, ask for a drink from me, a woman of Samaria?' (For Jews have no dealings with Samaritans.)*

With the use of a parenthetical statement, John reveals Jesus' true disposition. The real surprise wasn't that Jesus was talking down to her, rather, it was his willingness to speak to her at all. And remember, she took the request as a question, not a command.

The fact that she is not offended, but engaged, surprises us. Earlier, when making our initial sketch of her, we noted that the Jews had a longstanding disdain for Samaritans, and vice versa. Historically speaking, the split went back at least seven hundred years to the time of King Solomon's death and Israel's great divide into northern and southern kingdoms. The ten northern tribes, including the region of Samaria, abandoned Jerusalem as the center of religious activity. They began worshiping a multitude of gods at Mount Gerizim instead. And the intermarriage of those in the north with people from other nations and religions only served to deepen the rupture that existed on both sides.

So, as this conversation on relationship begins between Jesus (a Jew) and the woman (a Samaritan), it occurs within a highly charged unwritten code of silence that had already been in play for centuries. Animosity should have prevailed. This accounts for why the woman was surprised to hear Jesus speaking to her.

I wonder if Jesus' words might have triggered something else in her too. A longing perhaps? After all, when was the last time a man treated her with dignity and respect? She was used to being either the object of a man's lustful desire or his spiritual disdain. In breaking the silence, Jesus hints at *relationship*. He is beginning to find his way with her. The spiritual outsider? Yes. Could Jesus have something meaningful to offer this one who is seeking a relationship that lasts? Truth be told, we would like to think so, and not only for her sake. We long for relationships that matter. Just give us one that doesn't leave us feeling used at the end of the day.

PAST HURTS HINDER RELATIONSHIP

So, Jesus' opening words to the woman certainly don't hurt his chances of being well received. They might even give him a chance to reveal who he is and why he has come into the world, if that was his intent. But, if so, what Jesus says in response to the woman's question about why he would risk speaking to her definitely set him back:

> *Jesus answered her, 'If you knew the gift of God, and who it is that is saying to you, "Give me a drink," you would have asked him, and he would have given you living water.'*

> *The woman said to him, 'Sir, you have nothing to draw water with, and the well is deep. Where do you get that living water? Are you greater than our father Jacob? He gave us the well and drank from it himself, as did his sons and his livestock.'*

Listening in on this early moment in their conversation is painful. In these kinds of communications, misunderstandings abound and past hurts govern present responses. What is clear is this: This latest comment by Jesus set her off! And from our perspective, for good reason. She took Jesus' words to mean: 'Look woman, if you only knew how much I have to offer you, and if you only knew how awesome I am, you would have asked me to do something great for you.' We get the sense that Jesus just took two steps back, rather than one step forward.

From her vantage point, it is hard to imagine any other way to interpret his words. All she knows is that she had heard this kind of thing before. She's familiar with it. Arrogant men. Demeaning tone. Absolutely patriarchal, and in the worst sort of way. It only confirmed how she felt about the Jews of her day. Unsurprisingly then, she does what any strong woman would do, what any well-meaning dad would tell his daughter to do—she unleashes a comeback of her own: 'Yeah, right. You got water for me? I don't think so. You don't even have a bucket. Big southern man… You think you're greater than Jacob who gave us this well, huh?'

It might be worth taking a moment to consider why some people still respond to Jesus like this today. In our time, Jesus remains an anomaly. For all the print he gets on being loving, some feel he is uncharitable and unaware; not really a man with his feet on the ground. Like one who thinks he can do more for us than he really can. And as such, Jesus keeps us down simply by looking down on us. Can we really trust him with our wounded past? Is he aware of how complex our relational histories are? Let alone our present tangled ones? These questions need to be asked. For even if some people have no trouble with how the Bible shows him trumpeting on about his ability to give us *living water*, others among us are finding it hard enough to just *live and let live*, let alone be asked to decide on whether or not Jesus is worthy of all our loving.

Things look bleak for Jesus at this point in the conversation. The pain of this Samaritan woman was too deep and her history with men a thing too entrenched. Convincing her that these words were not intended to wound was going to be difficult. This conversation should be over. And on the outside chance that Jesus is who John says he is, he may have already squandered his opportunity with the woman at the well.

HOPES FOR RELATIONSHIP RENEWED

According to John, Jesus persevered.

> *Jesus said to her, 'Everyone who drinks of this water will be thirsty again, but whoever drinks of the water that I will give him will never be thirsty again. The*

water that I will give him will become in him a spring of water welling up to eternal life.'

It is as if Jesus said: 'Come on, I didn't have *this* water in mind. We both know that this well doesn't satisfy. And about Jacob, he was a great man. But give me a break, how great is someone who gives us something we still have to go get for ourselves every day? Hey, I'm like you. I'm sitting here exhausted too. What I meant was, I have something that comes from out of this world! It quenches real spiritual thirst. And I want to give it to you. What I have cultivates life. And besides, isn't that what you, and everybody in this dry and dusty part of the world, really want?'

Somehow, Jesus found words that encouraged her longing for something that wouldn't leave her empty. Something eternal. If we are honest with ourselves, we could use the same encouragement. It would be nice to possess something—an intimacy or a connection—

that didn't ultimately leave us empty, unsatisfied, and needing to return for more. A relationship with the God who created us for himself. A relationship that remains.

Suddenly, the woman at the well was now dreaming again. You might say Jesus provoked her spiritual thirst, her long-ago, pressed-down world of hurt, and she was wondering afresh if it might yet be satisfied. We know this, because she said:

> 'Sir, give me this water....'

Behind her beautifully hardened outward facade, this woman was all flesh and blood. She still longed for something beyond what this world had to offer. You and I weren't there to hear it, but I like to imagine the words coming off her lips nearly soundlessly in reflection.

BUT GUARDED STILL…

What I love about this woman at the well is that her heart and tongue are guarded still by her walls of reality. She knows she can't escape her actual lot in life. She began, 'Sir, give me this water,' but then she went on 'so that I will not be thirsty or have to come here to draw water.' The second half of her statement is important. After opening the door ever so slightly to the possibility of something greater, she seems to have caught herself. A protective shield has been raised to block the force of impending disappointment.

Peering at him now, through the narrow crack he has opened between her relationships here, and her longings for a better and everlasting relationship with God, she pauses. And by her words, she appears to be saying 'Sir, I desire that kind of water. Who doesn't? But to be honest with you, I don't believe it's out there anymore. Not for me anyway. I've got too much baggage. I've been through too much… Although, it sure would be nice if I didn't have to come here to get water every day.'

Here is someone who knows exactly who she is. And she is acutely aware of the world she lives in. Like ours, hers digs only solid wells—real ones—not imaginary ones. Wells whose bottoms contain nothing more than dry and useless dirt. In this world, relationships get busted. Bad things must be endured, and often alone. Truth be told, our past ventures for happiness through relationships have been met with one degree of failure or another. And that also includes the ones we never had, and aren't in now, but wish we were. For us, as it was for her, water, the *real water* of life's relational frustrations must be drawn every day.

PROOF THAT A BETTER RELATIONSHIP IS BEING OFFERED

Interestingly, Jesus isn't put off by her realism, just as I doubt he would be put off with ours. He is quite aware that the hopes he has rekindled in her through his words, require proof before they might become a reality in her life. And so, he simply presses on in an effort to make himself known.

> Jesus said to her, 'Go, call your husband, and come here.' The woman answered him, 'I have no husband.' Jesus said to her, 'You are right in saying, "I have no husband"; for you have had five husbands, and the one you now have is not your husband. What you have said is true.'

Can you imagine more provocative words than these? Things are more than personal now. Clearly, Jesus isn't talking about stone wells and dirty water. He is talking about life. *Her life*, with all its fragility and failure and embarrassment, with her multiple attempts at finding some sense of meaning through intimate relationships, has now been exposed.

We should pause. Her plight, namely that of being confined to seeking meaning in human relationships, only to come up empty, is common to us all. Other writers have picked up on this idea as well. *The Silence*, the third part of a celebrated trilogy from Swedish filmmaker Ingmar Bergman, illustrates this same predicament. While listening to a classical composition by Stravinsky, Bergman was reminded of a recent visit he made to a nineteenth-century cathedral. There, he had seen a stained-glass window depicting Jesus as the Good Shepherd. As the story goes, he stood before the shimmering portrait and called out: 'Speak to me.' No response. 'Speak to me,' he demanded again, 'I will not leave this place until you speak to me!' Jesus was again without words. Triumphant, Bergman left the cathedral. Later that same year, he wrote *The Silence*—which is about our failure to make a meaningful connection with God. One review of the film recalled 'the unnerving feeling that God has abandoned these characters to dubious salvation in their own connection.'[3]

Bergman was onto something. What would people do if God didn't exist? Or worse yet, what if he does exist, but doesn't have anything to say to us? Where would we turn if God was only present in shards of colored glass that adorn empty cathedrals?

We know where the woman went. In her search for a meaningful connection, she began to lower her spiritual gaze. Somewhere along the line she, like us, learned how to trade God for one another. But with the words, 'Go, call your husband, and come here,' Jesus had unmasked the futility of it all.

It is an uncomfortable moment. And it is so precisely because the conversation has turned so intimate. And yet, even here we sense that Jesus is not interested in humiliating her. It isn't about shame, but salvation. By raising the difficulties of her past, Jesus has left her no option but to look directly at her failures. She can't pretend or ignore or dissemble anymore. And I think that if we had been there, Jesus would have made us to do the same thing. He would tell us to 'Go, call your lovers, and come here'. Whether they be men or women. Many or few. Hidden or known. Same sex or not. John's Gospel implies that Jesus would know just what to say to us to prove that he has a better relationship to offer.

PROCESSING JESUS' OFFER…

The questions now rising before the woman at the well are important ones. Will she bring her relationships into his presence? Will she acknowledge her failures in pursuit of meaning? Will she take responsibility for drawing ultimate satisfaction from empty wells in dry ground? And if she is willing, will Jesus condemn her? Or us? Will he help or hurt? Put differently, if the woman at the well acts upon his word, if she runs to get her man and brings him to Jesus, can she trust him to show her how to make sense of things? And if so, will he provide her with a relationship that remains?

The woman at the well is now flush with the life-giving promise of fresh possibilities, but also with fear. Jesus has proven to her, beyond all doubt, that he knows her. 'Who is this man? How was he aware that I am living with another man? How did he know about the other five? We've never met. But, *he knows me*. He exposed my failures, and that was hard. But he also exposed my longing for a hope, a faith in something more, a salvation.'

What comes next in the conversation intrigues. Four things emerge. If Jesus can provide us with a better way, we need to consider the roles *place*, *spirit*, *truth*, and *Jesus* play in establishing a relationship with God.

THE IDEA OF 'PLACE' AND A RELATIONSHIP WITH GOD

For the first time, as her next words make clear, she now believes that Jesus might have something to offer her on a spiritual level. Not yet ready to collect her man, she is nevertheless ready to say:

> 'Sir, I perceive that you are a prophet. Our fathers worshipped on this mountain, but you say that in Jerusalem is the place where people ought to worship.'

Her statement that 'our fathers worshipped on this mountain' is a reference to Mount Gerizim, which would have been visible to them from the well. Still coyly protecting herself, she nevertheless now asks Jesus for advice on where to go to reconnect with God. Can she find God here, on this mountain? Or will she need to go all the way to Jerusalem? After all, both sites had a long history as centers for religious worship.

Her question marks an important moment in this conversation—for she is about to make the mistake many of us make. She thinks that she can transfer the faith she mistakenly put in relationships with other people, to the *places* which God is said to inhabit. In essence, she is asking: 'Do I start over with God by returning to the institutional services offered at the nearby mountain? Or, do I need to go and join the congregation in Jerusalem?' Intuitively, she wrongly believes (due to teachers who need a conversation with Jesus on religion) that *place* is significant when it comes to making a fresh start with God.

This is often the case for people today. When we decide to exchange our busted relationships for a better one, people think that merely by going to church services they can reconnect with God—as if *place* was the key factor in forging a sacred rapport. Others are trying to re-center themselves spiritually by finding some private internal soul *space* that brings them peace and a sense of spiritual peace. This too is faulty.

> *'Woman, believe me, the hour is coming when neither on this mountain nor in Jerusalem will you worship the Father.'*

What are we to make of this? Simply this: The relationship Jesus has to offer has little, if anything, to do with place. We won't find the intimacy we crave by simply returning to holy mountains, sacred cities, temple shrines, remote ashrams, immaculate churches, or any other sacred places of worship. They are not what establishes our relationship with God.

THE IDEA OF 'SPIRIT' AND A RELATIONSHIP WITH GOD

If Jesus doesn't want the woman at the well to travel the well-worn path of seeking the right *place* to establish her relationship with God, then what exactly does he have in mind? Fortunately, he tells her, and us:

> *'But the hour is coming, and is now here, when the true worshipers will worship the Father in spirit and truth, for the Father is seeking such people to worship him. God is spirit, and those who worship him must worship in spirit and truth.'*

According to Jesus, those of us who want to make a fresh start with God need to know something not only about *place*, but also the *spirit*.

It makes sense. Since the true God is himself a *spirit*, then we can only know him by worshiping him *in spirit*. In other words, outward acts of worship are not enough. An external devotion to a life of faith won't cut it. Getting up tomorrow morning and trying to turn over a new leaf by changing your habits and behavior and relationships is not the answer. Because of who he is, the thing God wants is worship *in spirit*.

Often, we hear people say: 'I am a practicing Christian,' or Jew, or Hindu, or Muslim. By the term *practicing,* people imply that faith is something we do. Jesus challenges this kind of language. He would have us come to know God in terms of who we are at our very core, in our *spirit*. If this is true, then establishing a relationship with God requires change from the inside out. We are to worship God from our inmost parts—from our *spirit*. And that is going to be a work that only God can bring about in us. Want God to do a fresh work in your life? Then ask him to give you his Spirit.

THE IDEA OF 'TRUTH' AND A RELATIONSHIP WITH GOD

The third idea Jesus put before the woman at the well is captured in the word *truth*. By this he simply means that our relationship to God must conform to that which is *true*. This teaching is highly contentious given the times in which we live. Evidently, the contemporary idea that God will accept our worship provided our *spirit* is wholeheartedly engaged and our faith commitments are *sincere* is unfounded. Sincerity isn't enough. And an intense *spiritual* interest isn't enough either. According to Jesus, a relationship that leads to eternal life must also be grounded in *truth* (see A Conversation with Jesus on Truth, where this idea is explored in depth).

Getting a grip on *truth* will prove challenging for each one of us. After all, the very idea that it exists has been largely discarded. We prefer to think that God accepts people without any discrimination at all. In fact, we often claim that no one has the upper hand on *truth*. Jesus would have us think otherwise.

Later in John's Gospel, we will hear Jesus say of himself: 'I am the way, and the *truth*, and the life. No one comes to the Father except through me.'4 This is the stunning claim of Christianity: Jesus, the one who holds out hope to us for a relationship with God, is the very truth by which we either enter into that relationship or not. So, to worship God aright must mean not only giving our lives over to Jesus, but living under the truthful word of Jesus. He is the way to reconnect with God. Are you ready to open yourself up to being changed by the truth of the word of Christ? That can be a scary thing.

BUT CONFUSED STILL…

Whatever Jesus said about *place, spirit, and truth* caught the woman by surprise. She wasn't guarded anymore. Just confused. She had asked what she thought was a simple question: 'Where do I go to find God?' And his layered response wasn't all that helpful. And so, with a growing sense of awkwardness, she does what we would have done. She says the first thing that comes to her mind.

> *'I know that Messiah is coming (he who is called Christ). When he comes, he will tell us all things.'*

In essence, she turned to this stranger and said: 'Well, I probably shouldn't have gotten into all this… I mean, you being a prophet and all. This isn't my area of expertise and I'm sure you're making the best effort you can to put it on the shelf where I can reach it. But, I'm not apparently up to it. I'm sure that when the Messiah comes, you know, God's great king,

I'm sure he will be able to clear things up for us outsiders.'

With these words, the climactic moment in her conversation with Jesus on relationships has arrived. For by speaking, she reveals that, deep down, even when confused, she is still holding to the hope that God will, one day, send his king into the world to clear it all up and rescue her from a million relational failures.

THE ROLE OF JESUS IN OUR RELATIONSHIP WITH GOD

With that hope now expressed in concrete words, with it all out there in the open, the woman is finally at a place in the conversation where Jesus can make himself known to her.

According to John, his next words are, 'I who speak to you am he.' That is, he says: 'I am the One who will clear all these things up for you. I am the Messiah—the Christ who makes the Father known—I am the relationship you have so badly been seeking and so desperately need.'

Jesus told her that he was the relationship for which she had been looking.

Jesus had come to do more than converse with her. He had come to save her from her sins, cover over her past mistakes, satisfy her deepest longings, pull her from the rubble of this world, and meaningfully re-establish her relationship with God. And amazingly, the woman began to believe him.

Now she was ready to go home and get her man and bring him to Jesus because she was convinced that Jesus could be trusted to sort things out. To make things right. To change things where needed, and when. She was ready to start living life under his every word. Here is how John puts it in his Gospel:

> So the woman left her water jar and went away into town and said to the people, 'Come, see a man who told me all that

I ever did. Can this be the Christ?' They went out of the town and were coming to him…. Many Samaritans from that town believed in him because of the woman's testimony, 'He told me all that I ever did.' So when the Samaritans came to him, they asked him to stay with them, and he stayed there two days. And many more believed because of his word. They said to the woman, 'It is no longer because of what you said that we believe, for we have heard for ourselves, and we know that this is indeed the Savior of the world.'

It isn't hard to imagine how this scene might play out on a Broadway stage. The set is now full. Dancing and parading around the well are countless men and women, and happy children too. Jesus is at ease in their midst. And he is speaking to each one in turn. He doesn't look exhausted anymore. Instead, he looks like a good shepherd—one who does speak, and who really does lead all his sheep to satisfying waters. Here comes one to him now. 'Jesus, will you speak to me?' He responds: 'Yes, of course I will. Come here my friend, sit down. Let's talk.' And with that the curtain begins to close to the joyful sounds of life abounding with laughter.

AND WHAT ABOUT YOU?...

Consequently, I now wonder, what will you do with Jesus? You know what the woman at the well did. She entered into a relationship with God, through Jesus, by believing what he said and with the assurance that he was what she had been looking for all along.

And you?

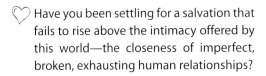 Have you been settling for a salvation that fails to rise above the intimacy offered by this world—the closeness of imperfect, broken, exhausting human relationships?

Is the water jar of your life empty and in constant need of refilling?

♡ Does your heart still long for something better, someone more satisfying?

♡ Do you desire to connect with God, but feel that you don't know quite where to start?

If so, simply follow the actions of the woman at the well. You won't be disappointed. You can have a fresh start. A relationship with God. Let me invite you to your own conversation with him by praying:

> *Our Heavenly Father, I believe that Jesus Christ is the One you sent into the world to speak for you. I desire something more from this life than what I now have. I confess that I have sinned against you by seeking meaning in relationships here, rather than in the one Jesus offers. He alone has the power to change me. Alter my spirit by giving me yours, and provide me with help to obey your truth as I learn to live under the word of Christ. In Jesus' name I pray, Amen.*

If you have prayed that prayer, I would encourage you to tell a Christian friend what you have done. Then, set out to find a Bible-teaching church that believes and teaches these things. They can help you grow.

JOHN 4:1-43

[1] *Now when Jesus learned that the Pharisees had heard that Jesus was making and baptizing more disciples than John* [2] *(although Jesus himself did not baptize, but only his disciples),* [3] *he left Judea and departed again for Galilee.* [4] *And he had to pass through Samaria.* [5] *So he came to a town of Samaria called Sychar, near the field that Jacob had given to his son Joseph.* [6] *Jacob's well was there; so Jesus, wearied as he was from his journey, was sitting beside the well. It was about the sixth hour.* [7] *A woman from Samaria came to draw water. Jesus said to her, 'Give me a drink.'* [8] *(For his disciples had gone away into the city to buy food.)* [9] *The Samaritan woman said to him, 'How is it that you, a Jew, ask for a drink from me, a woman of Samaria?' (For Jews have no dealings with Samaritans.)* [10] *Jesus answered her, 'If you knew the gift of God, and who it is that is saying to you, "Give me a drink," you would have asked him, and he would have given you living water.'* [11] *The woman said to him, 'Sir, you have nothing*

to draw water with, and the well is deep. Where do you get that living water? [12] Are you greater than our father Jacob? He gave us the well and drank from it himself, as did his sons and his livestock.' [13] Jesus said to her, 'Everyone who drinks of this water will be thirsty again, [14] but whoever drinks of the water that I will give him will never be thirsty again. The water that I will give him will become in him a spring of water welling up to eternal life.' [15] The woman said to him, 'Sir, give me this water, so that I will not be thirsty or have to come here to draw water.' [16] Jesus said to her, 'Go, call your husband, and come here.' [17] The woman answered him, 'I have no husband.' Jesus said to her, 'You are right in saying, "I have no husband"; [18] for you have had five husbands, and the one you now have is not your husband. What you have said is true.' [19] The woman said to him, 'Sir, I perceive that you are a prophet. [20] Our fathers worshiped on this mountain, but you say that in Jerusalem is the place where people ought to worship.' [21] Jesus said to her, 'Woman, believe me, the hour is coming when neither on this mountain nor in Jerusalem will you worship the Father. ²² You worship what you do not know; we worship what we know, for salvation is from the Jews. ²³ But the hour is coming, and is now here, when the true worshipers will worship the Father in spirit and truth, for the Father is seeking such people to worship him. ²⁴ God is spirit, and those who worship him must worship in spirit and truth.' ²⁵ The woman said to him, 'I know that Messiah is coming (he who is called Christ). When he comes, he will tell us all things.' ²⁶ Jesus said to her, 'I who speak to you am he.' ²⁷ Just then his disciples came back. They marveled that he was talking with a woman, but no one said, 'What do you seek?' or, 'Why are you talking with her?' ²⁸ So the woman left her water jar and went away into town and said to the people, ²⁹ 'Come, see a man who told me all that I ever did. Can this be the Christ?' ³⁰ They went out of the town and were coming to him. ³¹ Meanwhile the disciples were urging him, saying, 'Rabbi, eat.' ³² But he said to them, 'I have food to eat that you do not know about.' ³³ So the disciples said to one another, 'Has anyone brought him something to eat?' [34] Jesus said to them, 'My food is to do the will of him who sent me and to accomplish his work. [35] Do you not say, "There are yet four months, then comes the harvest"? Look, I tell you, lift up your eyes, and see that the fields are white for harvest. [36] Already the one who reaps is receiving wages and gathering fruit for eternal life, so that sower and reaper may rejoice together. [37] For here the saying holds true, "One sows and another reaps." [38] I sent you to reap that for which you did not labor. Others have labored, and you have entered into their labor.' [39] Many Samaritans from that town believed in him because of the woman's testimony, 'He told me all that I ever did.' [40] So when the Samaritans came to him, they asked him to stay with them, and he stayed there two days. [41] And many more believed because of his word. [42] They said to the woman, 'It is no longer because of what you said that we believe, for we have heard for ourselves, and we know that this is indeed the Savior of the world.' [43] After the two days he departed for Galilee.

ENDNOTES

1. August Wilson, *Joe Turner's Come and Gone* (New York: Theatre Communications Group, 2007), 29.

2. This woman's encounter with Jesus can be found in full by reading John 4:1-43. I encourage you to read it. The text can be found on pages 52-55. Unless otherwise marked, all subsequent quotations are from this passage.

3. Tom Keogh, 'The Silence.' Review of *The Ingmar Bergman Trilogy (Through a Glass Darkly, Winter Light, The Silence)*, directed by Ingmar Bergman. Review on Amazon.com. https://www.amazon.com/Bergman-Trilogy-Through-Criterion-Collection/dp/B0000A02TX. Accessed September 15, 2018.

4. John 14:6.

ALSO AVAILABLE:

A CONVERSATION

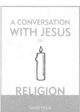

A CONVERSATION WITH JESUS ON RELIGION

9781527103245

A CONVERSATION WITH JESUS ON SUFFERING

9781527103269

A CONVERSATION WITH JESUS ON TRUTH

9781527103276

WITH **JESUS** SERIES

**A CONVERSATION
WITH JESUS ON
DOUBT**

9781527103283

**A CONVERSATION
WITH JESUS ON
HOPE**

9781527103290

**A CONVERSATION
WITH JESUS ON...
BOXSET**

9781527103238